Landscap

With my Easter blessings + thanks

Christina

'Enfolded in Love' series
General Editor: Robert Llewelyn

ENFOLDED IN LOVE (*Julian of Norwich*)
Robert Llewelyn

IN LOVE ENCLOSED (*Julian of Norwich*)
Robert Llewelyn

THE DART OF LONGING LOVE
('*The Cloud of Unknowing*')
Robert Llewelyn

AN ORATORY OF THE HEART (*Brother Lawrence*)
Robert Llewelyn

BY LOVE ALONE (*St Thérèse of Lisieux*)
Michael Hollings

THE DARKNESS OF FAITH (*Martin Luther*)
James Atkinson

THE DESERT OF THE HEART
(*The Desert Fathers*)
Benedicta Ward SLG

FIRE FROM A FLINT (*William Law*)
Robert Llewelyn and Edward Moss

THE HEART AT REST (*St Augustine*)
Dame Maura Sée OSB

THE HEART OF COMPASSION (*St Isaac of Syria*)
A. M. Allchin

LAMPS OF FIRE (*St John of the Cross*)
Sister Elizabeth Ruth ODC

LIVING WATER (*St Teresa of Avila*)
Sister Mary ODC

THE MIRROR OF LOVE (*Margery Kempe*)
Gillian Hawker

THRESHOLD OF LIGHT (*The Celtic Tradition*)
A. M. Allchin and Esther de Waal

LANDSCAPES OF GLORY

Daily Readings with Thomas Traherne

Introduced and edited by
A. M. Allchin

Darton, Longman and Todd
London

First published in 1989 by
Darton, Longman and Todd Ltd
89 Lillie Road, London SW6 1UD

Introduction and arrangement
© 1989 A. M. Allchin

British Library Cataloguing in Publication Data

Traherne, Thomas, *1637–1674*
    Landscapes of glory.
    1. Christian life – Devotional works
    I. Title   II. Allchin, A. M. (Arthur Macdonald), *193(*
    III. Series
    242

    ISBN 0–232–51860–2

Phototypeset by Input Typesetting Ltd
London SW19 8DR
Printed and bound in Great Britain by
Courier International Ltd, Tiptree, Essex

Contents

Acknowledgements   vi

Introduction   vii

Daily Readings with Thomas Traherne   1

Sources and index   61

Acknowledgements

Quotations from the Bodleian manuscript, *The Church's Year Book* (Eng. th. e. 51), are made by kind permission of the Bodleian Library, Oxford, and those from H. M. Margoliouth's edition of the *Thanksgivings* by kind permission of Oxford University Press.

Introduction

Thomas Traherne is usually known for a handful of striking passages in which he describes a childhood vision of a transfigured world, passages which have found their way into many anthologies. But there is more to Traherne than that. The passages in question need to be seen in the context of the whole work from which they come, *The Centuries of Meditations*, and that work needs to be seen in the context of Traherne's other writings. Up to the present it has been impossible to do this, for many of these writings remain unpublished.

Traherne is a writer whose work was hardly known in his own century. Only two books of his were published in his own time, one shortly before and the other shortly after his death in 1674. The works for which he is now famous, *The Centuries of Meditations*, and his poems, were totally unknown until they came to light and were published early in this century. Other writings of Traherne have come to light in the last twenty or thirty years. In the 1960s another book of meditations, *Select Meditations*, was discovered. More recently a much larger manuscript, *Commentaries of Heaven*, has been found. Neither of these has as yet been published.

In this selection I have made use both of *The Centuries of Meditations* and of the *Thanksgivings* which have been published but are not easily available. I have also used one of the unpublished manuscripts, a small volume in the Bodleian Library in Oxford called *The Church's Year Book*. Most of what is quoted from it here is being published for the first time. From another unpublished work, the *Select Meditations*, I have taken a passage (21) which seems to speak of the little church at Credenhill where Traherne was rector.

The story of this gradual discovery of more and more of Traherne's work is so strange and full of unlikely coincidences that one can hardly help wondering whether Traherne will not prove to be one of those writers who wrote more for subsequent ages than for his own. Like Julian of Norwich he was almost unknown in his own century. Perhaps like her, he will be found to have things to say to times much later than his own.

THE CHARACTER OF TRAHERNE

We know very little for certain about the outward facts of Traherne's life. He was born in 1637 in or near Hereford, the son of a shoemaker. His parents seem to have died while he was still young. In 1653 at the age of fifteen he became a student at Brasenose College in Oxford, taking his degree in 1656. In the following year he was appointed rector of the parish of Credenhill four miles north-west of Hereford. In 1660, on the restoration of the monarchy and of the episcopal order in the Church of England, Traherne was ordained and reappointed to Credenhill.

Sometime towards the end of the 1660s he became private chaplain to Sir Orlando Bridgeman, a prominent figure at the court of King Charles II, and it was at his house at Teddington that Traherne died in the autumn of 1674 at the age of thirty-seven.

While we have few details about Traherne's life, some things are certain. First, his Herefordshire origins. He was clearly a man with a great love for his native city and for the countryside around it. It features in his childhood memories and in some of the finest of his poems (8, 9). He was also evidently a man with a love of solitude and silence, and a great longing to explore the inner world of prayer and meditation (1).

In his day the Welsh-speaking districts of Herefordshire came to within a few miles of Hereford. Traherne must have known about Welsh even if he did not know it. He has many things in common with his contemporary Henry Vaughan who lived only thirty miles away to the west, near Brecon. Whether they ever met we do not know, but both men saw the poet's task as something holy, a calling to praise God in and through his whole creation. In this they were true, consciously or unconsciously, to the heart of the Celtic tradition.

But if Traherne was a country man, he was also a city-dweller. Oxford and London have a large part in his story. He shared in the interests and enthusiasms of his own time, among them the first beginnings of scientific inquiry. He read very widely and had a constantly active mind.

Like many others who love solitude, he also

loved company, and was evidently an eminently sociable and friendly person (40). In fact he had a devouring passion to communicate his vision to others and to share it with them. He was a great and attractive talker, and as we are now discovering, he was an indefatigable writer. The latest of his manuscripts to be discovered is 400 pages long!

JOY IN CREATION

The quality which strikes everyone who comes across the famous passages of Traherne's poetic prose is their joy and delight in God's creation (6, 7, 8, 9). It would not be fair to say that Traherne never lost this first joy of childhood. It is clear that he came to know times of grief and sadness, and in the more recently discovered writings there are signs of anxiety and disquiet. But something of that primal joy and delight remained with Traherne always. It is constantly recurring in his writings.

Others have spoken of this childhood vision, most notably William Wordsworth and in our own century Edwin Muir. We may wonder whether this is something given to few or whether in part it is a common experience, given to all, but which most of us have forgotten and lost under the weight of later impressions and confusions. Traherne seems to think it is a potential in us all.

Traherne is, foremost, a great proponent of the way of praise. 'Praise above all, for praise prevails', wrote Christopher Smart in eighteenth-century London. A hundred years earlier Traherne preached the same message. And like Smart, Traherne praises God in and through the whole creation. The Franciscan delight in the world of nature is to be found in times and places when St Francis was very little known.

It is clear that the childhood experience which Traherne recounts was difficult to adjust to the doctrine of original sin which was prevalent at his time. That was a doctrine which stressed the utter sinfulness of human nature, and saw the sin of Adam as something inherited by all his descendants.

Traherne seems to have thought, rather, that the fall was something which we each recapitulate in our own lives. After the first glimpse of Eden in our infancy, the early vision is clouded and lost. It can only be restored in Christ. Through it all, Traherne never altogether lost his sense of wonder and amazement before the goodness and glory of God revealed in his whole creation, and above all in the creation of humankind. With the psalmist he asks, 'What is man that thou art mindful of him, and the son of man that thou visitest him?' (Psalm 8:4).

Traherne had a very special love for the psalms and for all those passages in the Bible which speak about God's glory as revealed in creation. He tells us how he began to discover this strand in the biblical writings. 'As I read the Bible I was here and there surprised with such thoughts. . . Methought a new light darted in into all the psalms, and finally spread abroad over the whole Bible' (43, 44, 45, 46). In some of his Thanksgivings he weaves together the praises of the psalms with his own praises into an unforgettable tapestry (47, 49).

THE FULLNESS OF FAITH

In the end Traherne gives us a remarkably full and balanced vision of the Christian faith as it was understood and experienced by a priest of the Church of England at the end of the seventeenth century. As the manuscript called *The Church's Year Book* shows, he was a man with a great love for the Church's tradition of public worship and for the celebration of the feasts of the Church's year, as well as a love of inner meditation and prayer. In the festivals he found a way of renewing the first vision of Eden and anticipating the joys of heaven, for in them the world of eternity touches and redeems the world of time (50, 51, 52).

Nothing dims his ecstatic response to the goodness of God at work in all things. It is constantly renewed. But he does not stop there. He goes on to wonder at the love of God made known in the cross, which he sees as the central point of human history, and the central point of the whole of what God has made (14, 15, 16, 17). What would it have profited us to be born if we had not been redeemed?

But from the cross he goes on to the thought of the new life which comes with the resurrection and to all the gifts and graces which are ours in the coming of the Spirit at Pentecost. In *The Church's Year Book*, which covers the time from

Easter to All Saints' Day, he is particularly full in his meditations on the days from Ascension to Whitsunday. He calls the week before Whitsun the 'week of expectation' (34, 37, 38).

One particular aspect of his reflection here is very striking. He believed strongly that we are members one of another and that we find ourselves in and through one another. Perhaps like Charles Williams he had some special experience of this mysterious fact of coinherence. He seems to have had a special gift of friendship. He sees this as a gift of the Spirit who dwells within us in order that we may learn that we too dwell in one another (38).

In this same context of the coming of the Holy Spirit we find one of the most beautiful of his meditations, a kind of extended rumination on the quality of love as a gift of the Spirit. It is a love which brings joy and peace, a peace which can strengthen us through tribulation. It is a love which moves into acts of tenderness and compassion. It is a love which overflows into courtesy and generosity, and yet in the end thinks it has done nothing (29, 30, 31). Perhaps unconsciously in these passages Traherne is telling us something about himself. We hear that he was very generous to those in need. In his will he left his property in Hereford to provide almshouses for the poor.

One of the qualities in his writing which disconcerted his contemporaries was his insistence that all creation, all God's providence, all God's actions are made for *me*. It seems a little excessive, to say the least! But he is thinking of himself never in isolation from his fellow men and women. What belongs to each belongs to all. What belongs to all belongs to each.

Above all he encourages us to love, to love without measure, once our love is united with the love of God which sweetly orders all things. 'When we dote upon the perfections and beauties of some one creature, we do not love that too much, but other things too little. Never was any thing in this world loved too much, but many things have been loved in a false way, and all in too short a measure' (11).

TRAHERNE'S STYLE

Traherne wrote a very particular style which sometimes seems to us elaborate and ornate. I have now and then thought that reading too much of *The Centuries of Meditations* at once, is like trying to make a meal out of clotted cream. But it is without doubt a very beautiful style, and it is often used to remarkable effect.

It is generally agreed that he is greater as a prose writer than as a poet, though some of his poems are very fine. But they are not easy to fit into the pages of a book such as this one.

He can also be very simple and direct. 'It is in the nature of love to despise itself, and to think only of its beloved's welfare. Look to it, it is not right love that is otherwise. Moses and St Paul were no fools. God make me one of their number' (26).

He sometimes uses words in senses which are quite different from ours. Once or twice, I have changed them, for instance putting 'bring back' instead of 'reduce' and 'inseparable' instead of 'individual', when it was clear that the older meaning of the word was what he had in mind. But in general I have modernized only his spelling and his punctuation. His wording cannot be improved on. I have often shortened his lengthy paragraphs, and in a few cases have allowed a single meditation of Traherne to spread over three pages. In these cases each passage in this book can be read on its own, but they need to be taken together to have their full effect (29–31, 44–46, 50–52).

It is also wise to note that some of his favourite words were less familiar then than they are now, and so had a stronger meaning than they often do today. This is particularly the case with *enjoy*. When Traherne speaks of 'enjoying' ourselves in others, perhaps we might think of 'finding our joy' in others. When he speaks of enjoying the world aright, perhaps we might think of valuing the world aright as well as simply enjoying it.

TRAHERNE TODAY

In one of his essays Thomas Merton makes a comparison between Traherne and Julian of Norwich. He sees them as persons of vision who perceive the goodness of God present and at work in all things, and who convey in their writings a powerful sense of the optimism of grace and an assurance of God's love. May it be that Traherne, like Julian, is a writer whose hour has come? Certainly he speaks to us of a spirituality in which creation has a central place, and he is not afraid to thank God for the body as well as for the soul (58).

Another contemporary writer who makes use of the insights of Traherne is Melvyn Matthews. He speaks of Traherne's understanding of delight. 'Delight comes from a total acceptance of the gift of life. Gratitude and expectancy are its primary features. It is a discovery and a glad affirmation of the fact that the source of our lives comes from outside, that we do not have to make ourselves or achieve our own identity in any way.'

May this little book help many to discover anew their own God-given identity through a new apprehension of this liberating delight.

A. M. ALLCHIN

Note Those wishing to look further into Traherne's work, especially in its unpublished form, should consult the essays in *Profitable Wonders: Aspects of Thomas Traherne* (Amate Press, 14a Magdalen Road, Oxford, 1989).

A way of life

When I came into the country, and being seated among silent trees, had all my time in my own hands, I resolved to spend it all, whatever it cost me, in search of happiness, and to satiate that burning thirst which nature had enkindled in me from my youth. In which I was so resolute, that I chose rather to live upon ten pounds a year, and go in leather clothes, and feed upon bread and water so that I might have all my time clearly to myself, than to keep many thousands per annum in an estate of life where my time would be devoured in care and labour.

The praise of all creation

By an act of understanding therefore be present now with all the creatures among which you live, and hear them in their beings and operations praising God in an heavenly manner; some of them vocally, others in their ministry, all of them naturally and continually.

We infinitely wrong ourselves by laziness and confinement. All creatures in all nations and tongues and peoples praise God infinitely, and the more for being your sole and perfect treasures.

You are never what you ought till you go out of yourself and walk among them.

Questionings of childhood

Once I remember, I think I was about four years old, when I thus reasoned with myself, sitting in a little obscure room in my father's poor house, If there be a God, certainly he must be infinite in goodness.

And that I was prompted to, by a real whispering instinct of nature. And if he be infinite in goodness, and a perfect being in wisdom and love certainly he must do most glorious things, and give us infinite riches. How comes it to pass therefore that I am so poor? Of so scanty and narrow a fortune, enjoying few and obscure comforts?

I knew not then my soul or body, nor did I think of the heavens and the earth, the rivers and the stars, the sun or the moon. All these were lost and absent from me. But when I found them made out of nothing for me, then I had a God indeed, whom I could praise and rejoice in.

Enjoying the world aright

You never enjoy the world aright, till you see how a sand exhibiteth the wisdom and power of God, and prize in every thing the service which they do you in manifesting his glory and goodness to your soul far more than the visible beauty of their surface, or the material services they can do your body.

Your enjoyment of the world is never right till every morning you awake in heaven, see yourself in your Father's palace and look upon the skies and the earth and the air, as celestial joys, having such a reverend esteem of all, as if you were among the angels. The bride of a monarch, in her husband's chamber, hath no such causes of delight as you.

The sea flowing in your veins

You never enjoy the world aright, till the sea itself floweth in your veins, till you are clothed with the heavens, and crowned with the stars, and perceive yourself to be the sole heir of the whole world, and more than so, because men are in it who are every one sole heirs as well as you.

Till you can sing and rejoice and delight in God, as misers do in gold and kings in sceptres, you never enjoy the world.

Can you take too much joy in your Father's works? He is himself in every thing.

Some things are little on the outside and rough and common. But I remember the time, when the dust of the streets was as precious as gold to my infant eyes, and now it is more precious to the eye of reason.

The primal vision

Will you see the infancy of this sublime and celestial greatness? Those pure and virgin apprehensions I had from the womb, and that divine light wherewith I was born, are the best unto this day wherein I can see the universe. By the gift of God they attended me into the world, and by his special favour I remember them till now. Verily they seem the greatest gifts his wisdom could bestow, for without them all other gifts had been dead and vain. They are unattainable by book, and therefore I will teach them by experience. Pray for them earnestly, for they will make you angelical and wholly celestial.

Certainly Adam in paradise had not more sweet and curious apprehensions of the world than I when I was a child.

All things new and strange

All appeared new and strange at the first, inexpressibly rare and delightful and beautiful.

I was a little stranger which at my entrance into the world was saluted and surrounded with innumerable joys. My knowledge was divine. I knew by intuition those things which since my apostasy I collected again by the highest reason. My very ignorance was advantageous. I seemed as one brought into the estate of innocence.

All things were spotless and pure and glorious; yea, infinitely mine, and joyful and precious. I knew not that there were any sins, or complaints or laws. I dreamed not of poverties, contentions or vices. All tears and quarrels were hidden from mine eyes. Every thing was at rest, free and immortal.

I was entertained like an angel with the works of God in their splendour and glory. I saw all in the peace of Eden. Heaven and earth did sing my Creator's praises, and could not make more melody to Adam, than to me.

The world transfigured

The corn was orient and immortal wheat, which never should be reaped, nor was ever sown. I thought it had stood from everlasting to everlasting.

The dust and the stones of the street were as precious as gold. The gates were at first the end of the world.

The green trees when I saw them first through one of the gates transported and ravished me. Their sweetness and unusual beauty made my heart to leap, and almost mad with ecstasy, they were such strange and wonderful things.

The men; O what venerable and reverend creatures did the aged seem! Immortal cherubims! And young men glittering and sparkling angels, and maids strange seraphic pieces of life and beauty! Boys and girls tumbling in the street were moving jewels. I knew not that they were born or should die; but all things abided eternally as they were in their proper places.

Eternity was manifest in the light of day, and some thing infinite behind every thing appeared, which talked with my expectation and moved my desire.

All things were mine

The city seemed to stand in Eden, or to be built
in heaven. The streets were mine, the temple was
mine, the people were mine, their clothes and
gold and silver were mine, as much as their sparkling eyes, fair skins and ruddy faces. The skies
were mine, and so were the sun and moon and
stars, and all the world was mine and I the only
spectator and enjoyer of it.

I knew no churlish proprieties, nor bounds, nor
divisions, but all proprieties and divisions were
mine; all treasures and the possessors of them. So
that with much ado I was corrupted, and made to
learn the dirty devices of this world, which now
I unlearn and become as it were a little child again,
that I may enter into the Kingdom of God.

Two kinds of learning

Many men study the same things, which have not the taste of, nor delight in them, and their palates vary according to the ends at which they aim. He that studies polity, men and manners, merely that he may know how to behave himself and get honour in this world, has not the delight in his studies, as he that contemplates these things that he might see the ways of God among them, and walk in communion with him. The attainments of the one are narrow, the other grows a celestial king of all kingdoms. Kings minister unto him, temples are his own, thrones are his peculiar treasure.

He is nothing that knows these things merely for talk or idle speculation, or transient and external use. But he that knows them for value, and knows them his own, shall profit infinitely.

Nothing is loved too much

When we dote upon the perfections and beauties of some one creature, we do not love that too much, but other things too little.

Never was any thing in this world loved too much, but many things have been loved in a false way, and all in too short a measure.

The joy of God's love

It is an inestimable joy that I was raised out of nothing to see and enjoy this glorious world; it is a sacred gift whereby the children of men are made my treasures, but O thou who art fairer than the children of men, how great and inconceivable is the joy of thy love.

That I who was so lately raised out of the dust, have so great a friend, that I who in this life am born to mean things according to the world, should be called to inherit such great things in the way of heaven, such a Lord, so great a lover, such heavenly mysteries, such doings and such sufferings, with all the benefit and pleasure of them in thy intelligible Kingdom: it amazeth, it transporteth, it ravisheth me.

I will leave my father's house and come unto thee, for thou art my Lord and I will worship thee.

Grieving God's love

Lord, I lament and abhor myself that I have been the occasion of these thy sufferings. I had never known the dignity of my nature, hadst not thou esteemed it. I had never seen nor understood its glory hadst not thou assumed it. Be thou pleased to unite me unto thee in the bands of an inseparable love, that I may evermore live unto thee and live in thee.

O thou who wouldst never have permitted sin, hadst thou not known how to bring good out of evil, have pity upon me; hear my prayer. Let the remembrance of all the glory wherein I was created make me more serious and humble, more deep and penitent, more pure and holy before thee. And since the world is sprinkled with thy blood, and adorned with all kingdoms and ages for me, let me see thy glory in the preparation of them, and thy goodness in their government.

The cross

The cross is the abyss of wonders, the centre of desires, the school of virtues, the house of wisdom, the throne of love, the theatre of joys and the place of sorrows. It is the root of happiness and the gate of heaven.

The cross is the most exalted of all objects. It is an ensign lifted up for all nations, to it shall the Gentiles seek. His rest shall be glorious, the dispersed of Judah shall be gathered together to it, from the four corners of the earth.

If love be the weight of the soul, and its object the centre, all eyes and hearts may convert and turn unto this object, cleave unto this centre and by it enter into rest.

There we might see all nations assembled with their eyes and hearts upon it. There we may see God's goodness, wisdom and power, yea, his mercy and anger displayed. There we may see man's sin and his infinite value. There we might see the rock of ages and the joys of heaven. There we may see a man loving all the world and a God dying for mankind.

Jacob's ladder

The cross of Christ is the Jacob's ladder by which we ascend into the highest heavens.

There we see joyful patriarchs, expecting saints, and prophets ministering, apostles publishing and doctors teaching, all nations concentring, and angels praising.

That cross is a tree set on fire with invisible flame, that illuminateth all the world. The flame is love. The love in his bosom who died upon it. In the light of which we see how to possess all things in heaven and earth after his similitude.

His love unto all

Here you learn all patience, meekness, self-denial, courage, prudence, zeal, love, charity, contempt of the world, joy, penitence, contrition, modesty, fidelity, constancy, perseverance, holiness, contentment and thanksgiving, with whatsoever else is requisite for a man, a Christian or a king.

This man bleeding here was tutor to King Charles the martyr, and the great master of St Paul the convert who learned of him activity, and zeal unto all nations. Well therefore may we take up with this prospect and from hence behold all the things in heaven and earth.

Here we learn to imitate Jesus in his love unto all.

The image restored

And now, O Lord, heaven and earth are infinitely more valuable than they were before, being all bought with thy precious blood. And thou, O Jesus, art a treasure unto me far greater than all those. At what rate or measure shall I esteem thee!

Thou hast restored me again to the friendship of God, to the enjoyment of the world, to the hope of eternal glory, to the love of angels, cherubims and men, to the enjoyment and obedience of thy holy laws, which alone are sweeter to me than honey and the honeycomb, and more precious than thousands of gold and silver.

Thou hast restored me above all to the image of God. O let thy love be in me, that thy joy may be fulfilled in me for evermore.

The joy of redemption

Thou hast redeemed me,
  And therefore with hallelujahs
    Do I praise thy Name,
Recounting the ancient glories
  Which thou createdst in my soul,
    And confessing
That infinitely more is left unsaid.
  O my God,
    Sanctify me by thy Spirit,
    Make me a temple of the Holy Ghost,
    A willing person in the day of thy power.

The light of his countenance

Let my Saviour's incarnation be my exaltation,
  His death, my life, liberty and glory,
  His love, my strength,
    And the incentive of mine,
  His resurrection, my release,
  His ascension, my triumph,
  His Gospel, my joy,
  The light of his countenance
    (And of thine in him)
My { reviving / healing / comforting } Sun
In the day of thy grace, let me work for thy
    glory,
  Rejoice in thy goodness,
Living in thine image
  Towards all thy creatures.

Thy heart is with us

Thy glory, O Jesus, filleth the world.

Thou art ascended into heaven, but thy Spirit is among us, and thy heart is with us.

Thou hast not forsaken the earth. Thy charge is here and the pledge of thy love in the ministry of thy apostles.

Thy Church is the temple even here upon earth wherein thou dwellest.

How sweet it is to see the communion between thee and thy Church.

Thou mighty master of all the apostles, thou living root of all our confidence, to thee be glory for evermore.

The Church, hidden and revealed

When I see a little church environed with trees, how many things are there which mine eye discerneth not. The labour of them which in ancient ages builded it; the conversion of a kingdom to God from paganism, its protection by laws, its subjection to kings, its relation to bishops, its usefulness and convenience for the entertainment of Christians, the divine service, the office of ministry, solemn assemblies, praises and thanksgivings, for the sake of which it was permitted, is governed, standeth and flourisheth.

Perhaps when I look upon it, it is desolate and empty almost like a heap of stones, none of these things appearing to the eyes which nevertheless are the spiritual beauties which adorn and clothe it. The uses, relations, services and ends being the spiritual and invisible things that make any material to be of worth.

He who cannot see the invisible cannot enjoy nor value temples. But he that seeth them may esteem them all to be his own and wonder at the divine bounty for giving them so richly.

Knit together in godly love

My Lord, thou head of the holy catholic Church, I admire and praise thee for purchasing to thyself such a glorious bride, and for uniting us all by the blood of thy cross.

I beseech thee, let my love unto all be regular like thine, and pure and infinite. Make it divine and make it holy. And so make me to love all that I may be a blessing to all, and well pleasing to thee in all.

Teach me wisdom, how to expend my blood, estate, life and time in thy service for the good of all, and make all them that are round about me wise and holy as thou art. That we might all be knit together in godly love, and united in thy service to thy honour and glory.

The cross in all things

O Jesus, thou king of saints whom all adore, and the holy imitate, I admire the perfection of thy love in every soul.

Thou lovest every one wholly as if him alone, whose soul is so great an image of thine eternal Father that thou camest down from heaven to die for him, and to purchase mankind that they might be his treasures.

I admire to see thy cross in every understanding, thy passion in every memory, thy crown of thorns in every eye, and thy bleeding, naked, wounded body in every soul. Thy death liveth in every memory, thy crucified person is embalmed in every affection, thy pierced feet are bathed in every one's tears, thy blood droppeth on every soul.

Thou wholly communicatest thyself to every soul in all kingdoms, and art wholly seen in every saint, and wholly fed upon by every Christian. It is my privilege that I can enter with thee into every soul, and in every living temple of thy manhood and thy Godhead, behold again and enjoy thy glory.

To find life in death

Christ's body is not a cloud but a pillar assumed to manifest his love unto us. In these shades doth this sun break forth most oriently. In this death is his love painted in most lively colours.

God never showed himself more a God than when he appeared man. Never gained more glory than when he lost all glory, was never more sensible of our sad estate than when he was bereaved of all sense.

O let thy goodness shine in me! I will love all, O Lord, by thy grace assisting as thou doest, and in death itself will I find life, and in conquest victory.

Thus Samson by dying killed all his enemies, and then carried the gates of hell and death away, when being dead, himself was borne to his grave. Teach me, O Lord, these mysterious ascensions.

By descending into hell for the sake of others, let me ascend into the glory of thy highest heavens. Let the fidelity and efficacy of my love appear in all my care and suffering for thee.

Created for God's love

Love has a marvellous property of feeling in another. It can enjoy in another, as well as enjoy him. Love is an infinite treasure to its object, and its object is so to it.

God is love, and you are his object. You are created to be his love, and he is yours. He is happy in you, when you are happy, as parents in their children. He is afflicted in all your afflictions, and whosoever toucheth you toucheth the apple of his eye.

Will you not be happy in all his enjoyments? He feeleth in you, will not you feel in him?

In God you are crowned, in God you are concerned. In him you feel, in him you live, and move and have your being; in him you are blessed. Whatsoever therefore serveth him serveth you, and in him you inherit all things.

Moses and St Paul

'No man truly loves, unless he love another more than himself.' In ordinary instances this is apparent. If you come into an orchard with a person you love, and there be but one ripe cherry, you offer it to the other. If two lovers delight in the same piece of meat, either takes pleasure in the other, and more esteems the beloved's satisfaction. What ails men that they do not see it?

In greater cases this is evident. A mother runs upon a sword to save her beloved. A father leaps into the fire to fetch out his beloved. Love brought Christ from heaven to die for his beloved.

It is the nature of love to despise itself, and to think only of its beloved's welfare. Look to it, it is not right love that is otherwise. Moses and St Paul were no fools. God make me one of their number.

Love breaks in

Since love will thrust in itself as the greatest of all principles, let us at last willingly allow it room.

I was once a stranger to it, now I am familiar with it as with a daily acquaintance.

It is the only heir and benefactor of the world. It seems it will break in everywhere, as that without which the world could not be enjoyed. Nay, as that without which it would not be worthy to be enjoyed; for it was beautified by love, and commendeth the love of the donor to us.

Love is a phoenix that will revive in its own ashes, inherit death, and smell sweetly in the grave.

The joys and hazards of love

These two properties are in love, that it can attempt all and suffer all. And the more it suffers the more it is delighted, and the more it attempteth the more it is enriched, for it seems that all love is so mysterious, that there is something in it which needs expression, and can never be understood by any manifestation of itself, in itself, but only by mighty doings and sufferings.

This moved God the Father to create the world, and God the Son to die for it. Nor is this all. There are many other ways in which it manifests itself as well as these; there being still something infinite behind it; in its laws, in its tendernesses, in its provisions, in its caresses, in its joys as well as in its hazards, in its honour as well as in its cares. Nor does it ever cease till it has poured out itself in all its communications.

(i) The Spirit of love

Whosoever hath the Spirit, he must have love, and such a love as causeth joy, and such a joy as causeth peace; for love is concerned, and feeleth the happiness of another person.

He that hath a love universal and clear to God and man, enjoyeth the blessedness of God and man, and must therefore have joy, because God is blessed and the saints are happy, and himself is like God, great in love and the joy of all. All this rests in peace, tranquillity and contentment.

Because his greatness and felicity cannot be moved his happiness is supreme, in which he is satisfied, for no man can rest content, uncrowned. His content bringeth patience; for seeing his goodness immovable, and sovereign the divinity of his soul, and his treasures being secure, it makes him easily to bear afflictions, because God himself and his friends are happy, and all his tribulations are only in light and superficial things. His patience therefore springs not from necessity, but satisfaction, security, happiness and duty.

(ii) Love in action

Love moves him also to acts of mercy, tenderness and compassion, for he that is happy in love like God, knoweth the value of others' souls, and lamenteth the misery of other persons.

He is righteous and holy in seeking their welfare, and very courageous in rescuing them from dangers and bringing them light. And therefore is he longsuffering, because he pitieth their diseases and beareth their injuries, thirsting for their happiness.

He is great and unmovable, always abounding in the work of the Lord.

(iii) Love overflows with courtesy

How can he be unjust that loveth others as himself? Yes, he is liberal and overflows with courtesy; modest and humble, and after all thinks he hath done nothing, for love never remembereth the benefits it hath done, but is always bent upon doing more, yet is attended with an established confidence, because it injures no man, but is grateful to all.

Meekness is swallowed up in bounty and magnificence, and seemeth to be melted in compassion or buried in humility, yet is quickened by courage, and made resplendent in the activity of goodness, receiving injuries in silence and diligently returning innumerable blessings.

Sobriety and temperance and fear of offending are fruits naturally flowing from these. And they are all linked and woven together in piety to God and man.

Arteries of the Spirit

The means of grace are arteries to convey the Spirit to us.

Well may we hope if we use them well, that he will come unto us, to inform us by his holy word, to sanctify us by prayer, to comfort us in the sacraments.

These three, prayer, the word and the sacraments are a little trinity which God will bless.

A complete obedience in the conscientious use of his means never went away empty.

The fulfilment of God's promises

O holy Jesus, all the joys thou givest us in thy
birth, all the virtues thou givest us in thy resurrection, all the privileges and triumphs, gifts and
places thou givest us in thy ascension, are locked
up and sealed in this promise of the coming of the
Spirit, kept back and concealed from us till the
Holy Spirit unlock the same.

O shed abroad thy Spirit in our hearts, for in that
doth the fulfilling of all thy promises consist.

Unity in the Holy Spirit

We wait with thine apostles for the Holy Spirit.

O qualify us for his coming by giving us with the apostles unity in ourselves, unity in thy Church, unity with thee, that as unity tied God and man together, so it may unite thy Holy Spirit to us, and make him delight to dwell within us.

Make us to remember that as unity is the best preparation, so division is the greatest opposition to thy Holy Dove's coming upon us.

His Spirit is with us

He only has true knowledge who believes and practises what he knows. Be sure, therefore, O my soul, as thou growest wiser to grow better. Hear God's word well in his house, and do it in thine own. Remember and be sure to act as in the presence of the Holy Ghost.

Be always, I beseech thee, O Holy Spirit, near unto me, without me and within me, to bless all thy blessings to me, and to keep all evil from me.

Be with me, I beseech thee, to say grace at my meal, and in temperance at it.

Be with me in my prayers, and pray for me in my readings, that they may be profitable to me; in my meditations to apply them, in my words to direct them, in my good works to prosper them.

Be with me even in my failings, when my foot slippeth, to hold me up; in my errors to bring me back, in my sins to correct me, in my afflictions to support me, in all to sanctify me, and make me ever a willing person in the day of thy power.

Thyself the gift

O give thyself unto me, for without thee no gift at all can satisfy. And because thou thyself art the gift, O give me what thou art, that I may give thee what I am, and be made a partaker of the divine nature.

A perpetual Pentecost

It is a comfort to consider that the Holy Ghost did not descend this day for the apostles only but for all men, so that if we be concentred all in one place, in unity, verity and concord, in one faith and one Church, he shall fill us with his gifts and give us utterance of them in our lives and conversation.

He that loves prayer so fervently that in prayer he feels the vehemence and fire of the Holy Ghost, dwells in an everlasting Whitsunday with God almighty.

The sharing of gifts

He came in tongues to give them utterance to distribute the benefit which they themselves enjoy, and to communicate his gifts.

And therefore is contention the most pernicious thing in the whole world, because this division of tongues was intended for union, for by communicating ourselves we are united to others, give others the benefit of ourselves, and enjoy ourselves in being enjoyed.

By communicating ourselves we fill others, by filling others we live in them, by living in them we feel in them, see and enjoy whatever they have and are.

So dwelling in each other the Holy Ghost dwelleth in both, enjoying both and making both a benefit to the other.

And thereby he attaineth the end which his nature desireth, and for which he cometh, which is to unite two, that he might be glorified in either, for the sake of either.

Since therefore this division of tongues is not for contention, but communication, mixture and union, how infinitely are they to blame who use their tongues for dissipation and division, or alienation and schism; for all coldness is in destructive separation.

Withdrawal and return

One may not be so given to contemplation as to forget the good of one's neighbour, nor so given over to action as to forget divine speculation.

Our saviour Jesus lived a life in public, sociable, humane, charitable, free and common. And yet, for opportunity of special devotion, retired to prayer and contemplation.

It was in solitude that he kept his fasts. Rocks and mountains heard his prayers. Among beasts was he born, and in the wilderness he fed his thousands. Upon a mountain he prayed, upon a mountain he was transfigured, upon a mountain he died, to a mountain in Galilee he invited his disciples, and from a mountain he ascended.

In which retirements his devotions received a great advantage of freedom from distractions. So that solitude is a good school to learn piety and virtue in, and the world the best theatre to practise it.

A lover of company

Thou, Lord, hast made thy servant a sociable creature; for which I praise thy name,
    A lover of company, a delighter in equals;
    Replenish the inclination, which thyself hast implanted.

O Lord, I delight in thee
For making my soul so wholly active,
    So prone to employment
    So apt to love,
That it can never rest, nor cease from thinking.
    I praise thee with joy
For making it so wide that it can treasure ages,
    See thine eternity
    And walk with thee in all thy ways.

The world in a grain of sand

Suppose a river or a drop of water, an apple or a sand, an ear of corn, or an herb; God knoweth infinite excellencies in it more than we. He seeth how it relateth to angels and men, how it proceedeth from the most perfect lover to the most perfectly beloved, how it representeth all his attributes. God the author and God the end is to be beloved in it. Angels and men are to be beloved in it, and it is to be highly esteemed for their sakes.

O, what a treasure is every sand when truly understood! Who can love any thing that God hath made too much? His infinite goodness and wisdom and power and glory are in it.

God in his creation

Upon this I began to believe that all other creatures were such that God was himself in their creation, that is *Almighty power wholly exerted*. And that every creature is indeed as it seemed in my infancy, not as it is commonly apprehended. Every thing being sublimely rich and great and glorious.

Every spire of grass is the work of his hand, and I in a world where every thing is mine, and far better than the greater sort of children esteem diamonds and pearls; gold and silver being the very refuse of nature, and the worst thing in God's Kingdom. Howbeit truly good in their proper places.

New light on the Scriptures

Little did I imagine that while I was thinking these things I was conversing with God. I was so ignorant that I did not think any man in the world had had such thoughts before. Seeing them therefore so amiable, I wondered not a little, that nothing was spoken of them in former ages.

But as I read the Bible I was here and there surprised with such thoughts, and found by degrees that these things had been written before, not only in the Scriptures but in many of the fathers, and that this was the way of communion with God in all saints, as I saw clearly in the person of David.

Methought a new light darted in into all his psalms, and finally spread abroad over the whole Bible. So that things which for their obscurity I thought not in being were there contained; things which for their greatness were incredible were made evident, and things obscure, plain. God by this means bringing me into the very heart of his Kingdom.

(i) The glory of man

That hymn of David in the eighth psalm was supposed to be made by night, wherein he celebrateth the works of God; because he mentioneth the moon and stars, but not the sun in his meditation. 'When I consider the heavens which thou hast made, the moon and the stars which are the works of thy fingers, What is man that thou art mindful of him, or the son of man that thou visitest him? Thou madest him a little lower than the angels, and hast crowned him with glory and honour. Thou hast given him dominion over the works of thy hands.'

This glory and honour wherewith man is crowned ought to affect every person that is grateful with celestial joy, and so much the rather, because it is every man's proper and sole inheritance.

(ii) The mirror of God's glory

See how in the sixty-fifth psalm he introduceth the meditation of God's visible works sweetly into the tabernacle and maketh them to be the fatness of his house, even of his holy temple.

God is seen when his love is manifested, God is enjoyed when his love is prized.

When we see the glory of his wisdom and goodness, and his power exerted, then we see his glory. And these things we cannot see till we see their works.

When therefore we see God's works, in them as in a mirror we see his glory.

(iii) The old made new

In his other psalms he proceedeth to speak of the works of God over and over again; sometimes stirring up all creatures to praise God for the very delight he took in their admirable perfection, sometimes showing God's goodness and mercy by them, and sometimes rejoicing himself and triumphing in them.

In the one hundred and third psalm he openeth the nature of God's present mercies, both towards himself in particular and towards all in general, turning emergencies in this world into celestial joys.

In the one hundred and fourth psalm he insisteth wholly upon the beauty of God's works in creation, making all things in heaven and earth, and in the heaven of heavens, in the wilderness and the sea, his private and personal delights.

In the one hundred and fifth, and one hundred and sixth psalms he celebrateth the ways of God in former ages with as much vehemency, zeal and pleasure as if they were new things, and as if he were present with them seeing their beauty and tasting their delight that very moment.

Awake, my heart

O that my heart were awake, O God,
 To see the glory of thy handiwork.
 Thy visible works are
  The joy of angels
  The delight of cherubims
  Heavenly treasures.
When thou hadst laid the foundations of the
earth, and accomplished the creation of the world,
 The morning stars sang together and all the
sons of God shouted for joy.
 Blessed be the glory of him who created all
things, and upholdeth them daily by the word of
his power.
 All these thy goodness giveth me
 Which I with Moses and thy saints enjoy.

The communion of saints

I bless thy name for the perfection of thy goodness so wholly communicable to many thousands;
   So endlessly communicated from all gener-
ations, coasts, and regions to every soul.
   By inviting whom thou invitest me

Because they are my $\left\{\begin{array}{l}\text{friends}\\ \text{temples}\\ \text{treasures}\end{array}\right.$

     And I am theirs
   Delighted by my love in all their happiness.
   He hath chained ages and kingdoms together
     Nor can they without us
     Nor we without them
       Be made perfect.

With angels and archangels

Bless the Lord, O my soul, and all that is within me bless his holy name.

Bless the Lord, O my soul, and forget not all his benefits.

O Lord who art clothed with majesty,
    My desire is, to praise thee.
    With the holy angels and archangels
        to glorify thee.
And with all the saints in the Church
    triumphant
    For the eternal brightness
    Of thine infinite bounty,
    The freedom of thy love
Wherein thou excellest the beams of the sun
    To celebrate thee.

(i) Heaven upon earth

Why should we not spend some time upon holy days in contemplating the beauty of holy days in themselves?

They are the ornaments of time and the beauty of the world,

The days of heaven seen upon earth,

The seasons of melody, joy and thanksgiving

The lucid intervals and lights of the year

The relics of Eden and superadded treasures,

A grateful relaxation from cares and labours,

The very cream and crown and repose of our lives,

Wherein we antedate the resurrection of the dead

And come from our shops to our Saviour's throne,

From ploughing our fields to manna in the wilderness

From dressing our vineyards to the wine of angels

From caring for our children, to be the sons of God.

(ii) God's open house

They are spiritual regions, wherein we walk in the paths of God.

Market days of heaven,

Appointed seasons, wherein God keepeth open house,

And blessed opportunities wherein we come from our solitary closets to see ourselves in solemn assemblies.

Single devotions are weak in comparison of these; here is the joy and strength of union.

A private person is but half himself; and is naturally magnified in others.

He is enlarged and multiplied when he sees himself in so many faces in divine assemblies.

The difference between earth and heaven is that here we are dispersed, there we shall ever be united together.

(iii) Landscapes of glory

These days are tastes and sure earnests of our eternal rest,

Wherein we enter the temple as the school of Christ.

They are mysterious opportunities, diffusing our souls and elevating them to heaven,

Landscapes of glory,

Golden links uniting our souls and all things together.

Apostles, prophets, patriarchs appear in them and come unto us.

Moses, King David, and Solomon welcome us,

Saints and martyrs visit us.

Without contemplation we lose the benefit of the ages, and without such days the benefit of contemplation.

The king's exchequer is laid open, and the doors are open into all his treasures.

Without sanctifying these we lose the benefit and the end of our lives, which is to enter into the treasuries of God almighty, and to feel his love, and to offer up ourselves in joy and thanksgivings.

The angels assist us

Most Holy God, and author of all sanctity and lover of all unity, whose wisdom hath established an admirable communion between the Church triumphant in heaven and militant on earth. Mercifully grant that as thy blessed angels pray to thee for us, we may praise thee continually for them, and in correspondence with their perfect charity, with a pious affection celebrate their memory, till we all meet before thy glorious throne, to adore with one heart the Saviour of us all, who with thee and the Holy Ghost liveth and reigneth ever one God, world without end. Amen.

A threefold love

In all love there is a love begetting, a love begotten, and a love proceeding. Which though they are one in essence, subsist nevertheless in three several manners. For love is benevolent affection to another; which is of itself and by itself relateth to its object. It floweth from itself and resteth in its object.

Love proceedeth of necessity from itself, for unless it be of itself it is not love. The love from which it floweth is the fountain of love; the love which streameth from it is the communication of love, or love communicated, and the love which resteth in the object is the love which streameth to it. So that in all love the Trinity is clear.

Love in the fountain

Love in the fountain and love in the stream are both the same. And therefore are they both equal in time and glory. For love communicateth itself, and therefore love in the fountain is the very love communicated to its object.

Love in the fountain is love in the stream, and love in the stream is equally glorious with love in the fountain. Though it streameth to its object it abideth in the lover, and is the love of the lover.

The fullness that filleth all in all

The omnipresence and the eternity of God are our throne, wherein we are to reign for evermore.

His infinite and eternal love are the borders of it, which everywhere we are to meet, and everywhere we are to see for evermore.

In this throne our Saviour sitteth, who is the alpha and omega, the first and the last, the Amen and the faithful witness, who said, The glory which thou hast given me I have given them, that they may be one as we are one. In him the fullness of the Godhead dwelleth bodily.

If that be too great to be applied to men, remember what follows, his Church is the fullness of him that filleth all in all.

The fullness of the Godhead dwelleth in him for our sakes.

To rest in God

O infinite God, centre of my soul, convert me powerfully unto thee, that in thee I may take rest, for thou didst make me for thee, and my heart is unquiet till it be united to thee.

And seeing, O eternal Father, thou didst create me that I might love thee as a son, give me grace that I may love thee as my Father.

O only begotten Son of God, redeemer of the world, seeing thou didst create and redeem me that I might obey and imitate thee, make me to obey and imitate thee in all thy imitable perfections.

O Holy Ghost, seeing thou didst create me to sanctify me, do it, O do it for thine own glory; that I may acceptably praise and serve the holy and undivided Trinity in Unity and Unity in Trinity. Amen.

The praise of heaven and earth

Let all thy creatures bless thee, O Lord, and my soul praise and bless thee for them all.

I give thee thanks for the being thou givest unto the heavens, sun, moon, stars, and elements; to beasts, plants, and all other bodies of the earth; to the fowls of the air, the fishes of the sea.

I give thee thanks for the beauty of colours, for the harmony of sounds, for the pleasantness of odours, for the sweetness of food, for the warmth and softness of our raiment, and for all my five senses, and all the pores of my body, so curiously made, and for the preservation as well as use of all my limbs and senses.

Above all, I praise thee for manifesting thyself unto me, whereby I am made capable to praise and magnify thy name for evermore.

The love of Jesus Christ

The world serves you, as it teaches you more abundantly to prize the love of Jesus Christ. For since the inheritance is so great to which you are restored, and no less than the whole world is the benefit of your Saviour's love, how much more are you to admire that person that redeemed you from the lowest hell to the fruition of it? Your forfeiture was immeasurable and your sin infinite, your despair insupportable and your danger eternal.

How happy are you therefore that have so great a Lord whose love rescued you from the extremest misery. It is a heavenly thing to understand his love and see it well.

Prayer

O eternal wisdom instruct me,
O eternal light illuminate me,
O eternal purity cleanse me,
O thou omnipresent power strengthen me,
O infinite holiness sanctify me,
Immutable love establish me,
Eternal mercy have mercy on me.

Sources and index

The figures in bold type refer to the pages of Readings in this book. They are followed by the Sources.

The source references which contain a roman number followed by an arabic number, e.g. III.46, refer to *The Centuries of Meditations*, which have been published in several editions. Those which are preceded by a *T* refer to the pages in volume II of H. M. Margoliouth's edition of the *Thanksgivings* (Oxford 1958). Those which contain an arabic number alone refer to the pages in the Bodleian MS. *The Church's Year Book*. The single reference to the *Select Meditations* (unpublished) has the abbreviation *SM*.

1	III.46	**17**	I.76
2	II.76	**18**	*T* 242
3	III.16	**19**	*T* 242–3
4	I.27, 28	**20**	80
5	I.29, 25	**21**	*SM* III.83
6	III.1	**22**	I.79
7	III.2	**23**	I.86
8	III.3	**24**	I.90
9	III.3	**25**	I.52
10	III.41	**26**	IV.56
11	II.66	**27**	IV.61
12	I.92	**28**	IV.62
13	I.78	**29**	53
14	I.58, 59	**30**	54
15	I.60	**31**	54
16	I.61	**32**	54

33	43	**47**	*T* 247
34	43	**48**	*T* 297
35	54	**49**	*T* 214
36	44	**50**	100
37	53	**51**	100
38	51	**52**	101
39	73	**53**	97
40	*T* 326, 284	**54**	II.40
41	II.67	**55**	II.41
42	III.62	**56**	IV.72
43	III.66	**57**	*T* 228
44	III.71	**58**	*T* 228–9
45	III.86	**59**	II.95
46	III.92	**60**	112